Roger Trigg is   he
University of   at
the Ian Ramsey   or
of many books on philosophy, his latest is *Beyond Matter: Why Science Needs Metaphysics*.

James 'faith w/o works is dead'

What are 'works' –

What is the cause that takes
precedence over all things?

Paul: works / faith
___ : justification by faith

works – demonstrations of the
         Jewish Law

Little Books of Guidance

Finding answers to life's big questions!

Also in the series:

DOES SCIENCE UNDERMINE FAITH?

A little book of guidance

ROGER TRIGG

First published in Great Britain in 2018

Society for Promoting Christian Knowledge
36 Causton Street
London SW1P 4ST
www.spck.org.uk

Copyright © Roger Trigg 2018

All rights reserved. No part of this book may be reproduced or transmitted
in any form or by any means, electronic or mechanical, including
photocopying, recording, or by any information storage and retrieval system,
without permission in writing from the publisher.

SPCK does not necessarily endorse the individual views contained in its
publications.

British Library Cataloguing-in-Publication Data
A catalogue record for this book is available from the British Library

ISBN 978–0–281–07868–4
eBook ISBN 978–0–281–07869–1

Typeset by Manila Typesetting Company
First printed in Great Britain by Ashford Colour Press
Subsequently digitally reprinted in Great Britain
eBook by Manila Typesetting Company

Produced on paper from sustainable forests

Contents

1

Does science disprove God?

Scientific dogmatism

In the contemporary world, reason is often thought to be the preserve of scientists. They sometimes seem to claim a monopoly on establishing what is true, or even credible. This view has a major influence on public life, and it is all too easy for non-scientific ideas, such as a belief in God, to be dismissed as irrational, and have no right to a voice in public affairs. All this must be challenged.

'If it isn't science, it's fiction.' So read a placard in a contemporary March for Science in Washington DC, replicated in major cities around the world. Thus what cannot be demonstrated, or even proved, in a scientific laboratory, is in the strictest sense of the term false. It is mere storytelling. The claim is that science reigns supreme and is the only way of discovering truth. It alone provides us with knowledge. The very term 'science' comes from the Latin *scientia*, for knowledge. Yet in recent generations, at least in English, the word has been narrowed to mean empirical science, the kind of knowledge obtained exclusively through human experience in observation and experiment. Not long ago, it was used much more widely.

Philosophy was studied until recently under the description the 'Moral Sciences' in Cambridge University. Theology was once called the 'Queen of the Sciences'. In current German, the word *Wissenschaft* means knowledge gained more widely than just through the methods of empirical science. A Philosophy Congress can thus be described by Germans, even in English, as a 'Scientific Congress'.

How has the word 'science' been narrowed to imply that experimental science is the *only* path to truth? Vast tracts of human experience, then, have nothing to do with what is true. Theories of goodness, beauty, or what is right, become just 'fiction'. They become stories we choose to live by with no universal validity, and no claim to reflect the world as it is. Reference to religious faith in general, and to Christian faith in particular, is regarded as mere storytelling. People's faith may be real enough in that they genuinely live in accord with certain beliefs. That, though, seemingly has no bearing on what other people might choose to live by, let alone what they ought to. If truth is established by science alone, your or my choice of a way of life is a matter of arbitrary commitment. What Christian faith points to, namely trust in God as the Creator and Source of everything, is regarded as beyond the reach of human science. It is not to be taken seriously as a claim to be an account of what there is, since the latter is defined by science alone.

These sweeping statements have their roots in philosophy current in the middle of the twentieth century. A circle of philosophers meeting in Vienna[1] before the Second World War made much of what they termed the 'scientific world-conception'. They believed that 'the scientific outlook knows no insoluble riddle'. This meant simply that what could not be explained by science was to be discarded as meaningless. A. J. Ayer popularized this approach in Britain with his book *Language, Truth and Logic.* Following the Vienna Circle, he tied not just truth but also meaning to scientific verification. What a scientist could not find out was not real. If I say to you that there is a 'heffalump' in my garden, and you want to go and see it, I may deny that it is visible. I may even be unable to describe what it would be like if you could see it. You may well come to the conclusion that a hef-falump that cannot be discovered, or even described, is not so different from no heffalump at all. The word does not gain any grip on the real world. The contention of those, like Ayer, who made scientific evidence the standard of meaning and truth was that statements beyond the reach of science, such as those about God, were in as bad a position as those about heffalumps. They could not grasp what was real, simply because reality was defined as that which was within the reach of science.

Like the demonstrators who proclaim that all is fiction without science, anyone asserting that the sciences are the source of all knowledge, and the sole criteria of what is true, must face the charge of irrational dogmatism. The very announcement that all is fiction beyond science is not itself a scientific statement. It is a statement *about* science, its scope and limits, and not one within science. It cannot be seen to be true in a laboratory. The conclusion must be that it itself is a piece of fiction.

Science is an impressive product of human reason. It seems to show how we are able to reach out beyond our prejudices, and come to see how the world really works. Yet we only trust science because we have a prior trust in the capabilities of human rationality. We see the importance of science and its proven methods of testing theories through observation and experiment. This is because we can stand outside science. We see its achievements and its ability to progress. Science cannot justify itself, and to think that all reasoning can only take place within science is self-defeating.

If someone alleges that science can explain everything, they cannot mean that we know everything now. It would be ridiculous to suggest that anything outside the current reach of scientific theory does not exist. Current science is a product of humans, who are limited in their capabilities. No one is omniscient. All make mistakes, and the human ability to observe and experiment is limited by the constraints of space and time. When A. J. Ayer was teaching philosophy in the Oxford of the 1960s, no one had gone round the moon or seen the other side. So-called verificationists, who wanted to link reality and a human ability to verify through science, were genuinely concerned about what was meant by the reality of the other side of the moon when no one could see it. They had to extend the idea of verification and falsification to what could *in principle* be verified or falsified. They could imagine what it would be like to go round the moon, and soon cosmonauts did.

The limits of science

Vast tracts of the universe lie beyond our ability in principle to observe them, just as there are quantum events at microscopic level beyond the capability of our instruments to

4

measure. As a result, scientists, particularly in physics, have come to recognize the reality of entities, both large and very small, that we can never see, and may perhaps be always inaccessible. The role of theory in science, going far beyond the baseline of observation and experiment, has been stressed more and more in the philosophy of science over the last 50 years. The burning contemporary question is how far physics can stray from what we can in principle test, and still count its subject matter as scientific, rather than going *beyond* science into so-called 'metaphysics'. Some physicists quite seriously want to talk about many universes, even an infinite number, all of which are by definition beyond our reach and may have different, even unimaginable, physical laws. Yet why should talk of such universes, so different from our own that their nature is inconceivable to us, be regarded as more within the scope of rational explanation than a God who is the source and grounding of everything? Saying that the one is scientific and rational, but that reference to God is irrational because unscientific, seems arbitrary, if not inconsistent.

Any attempt to tie truth to the operation of science has to face the question of whether we are going to rely on science as it is today or science as it might one day be. We can certainly, even in scientific terms, envisage realities removed from our own immediate reach. Otherwise we could make no sense of scientific progress, since we could never discover anything new. We have to recognize the provisional nature of science, and the inadequacy of much of the evidence at present available to us. That motivates us to stretch scientific boundaries, even if we have to produce the relevant technology to give us new information. That has happened in the past, such as in the seventeenth century when telescopes and microscopes extended our reach as human beings, a process that has continued today with our use of satellites and other methods of penetrating outer space. Even so, physical reality will always outstrip our ability to observe it, even with the most sophisticated equipment. As human beings, we are limited by our place in space and time, so what there is and how far we can know it have to be distinct notions. The mysterious nature of physical reality drives the scientific urge to find out more. The idea that science could be in a position to understand everything makes the erroneous assumption that everything is accessible to human experience.

We might still be tempted to say that reality is defined by some ideal science. Even if we could achieve full knowledge of all conceivable facts, that future science is as far removed from our present life as the idea of a reality that is dismissed by scientists as metaphysical. Even if we hope to understand through mathematics the principles on which the whole universe operates, that does not mean that we are defining reality through our knowledge. When we try to comprehend a reality that operates independently of us, we discover its nature. We do not construct it. Otherwise science itself would be fiction.

That reality is the same for everyone, and so science, when successful, has universal validity. It gains its authority because it is recognized that there is no such thing as Western science or Chinese science. Observations made in Beijing are valid in Washington DC, or London, or vice versa. We live in one world, the nature of which constrains all humans whatever their culture. Given the diversity of human belief in religious and other matters, this makes science, with its methods of empirical investigation and peer review, seem all the more impressive. Many look to the agreement that appears possible in scientific investigation, and compare it unfavourably with the cacophony of religious disagreement around the world. Some think that the calm rationality of science might provide humans with the way through their quarrels and disagreements. 'Facts' and 'evidence' will force us all to agree.

Yet what are the scientific facts? One of the developments in the history and philosophy of science over the last 50 years has been the growing realization that data do not come labelled as 'facts'. Consider Sherlock Holmes looking in a garden for clues about an intruder. He will not find labels on a dropped piece of paper or a footprint saying 'clue'. What he regards as significant and enlightening will depend on what he regards as relevant to his investigation. It all depends on his theory. Anyone else looking at the same garden would not notice the same things. It is the same in science. One idea about science was that it consisted of the mind passively collecting data like a sponge. Musty old museums, with ranks of cabinets containing curiosities seemingly unrelated by any theme, exemplified this. Sir Karl Popper, the noted philosopher of science, ridiculed the idea as 'the bucket theory of the mind'. Human beings in general, and scientists in particular, have to be active agents in the world. They cannot pick out what is relevant for their purposes, without a theory tying things together. What once appeared literally as mere background noise to physicists studying the universe became recognized as background radiation from the Big Bang at the beginning of our universe. All that was needed was a theory to demonstrate its significance. The cosmic microwave radiation picked up by instruments in 1963 was first thought to be interference caused by pigeon droppings on the antennae of the equipment. Facts have to be identified as such by scientific theory, which can take note of them and make sense of them.

Even so, too much should not be made of the priority of theory. It could imply that truth is simply the product of such theory, so that what there is depends on what we are looking for. The world as posited in one scientific theory may seem very different from that posited in another. Scientists, it has been said,[2] then live in different worlds, so that when they adopt a new theory, they live in a new world. (An example would be the change from classical mechanics to quantum mechanics.). The opposing, and surely correct, view is that we all live in the same world and gradually find out more about an actual reality. Scientists do not create different ones for themselves and their colleagues.

The provisional character of science

The fact that the world as seen by physicists at the end of the nineteenth century was radically different from that seen through the lens of quantum physics raises an issue. Does it mean that classical physics was mistaken in what it thought it knew? If scientists could be so misguided, might not present-day scientists be equally deficient in their understanding? Can we rely on science at all? Some would allege that science just reflects the prejudices and preoccupations of the society that produced it. Far from explaining everything, it does not explain anything. The idea of a persisting scientific truth and rock-solid scientific facts seems very far from what actually happens in the course of the history of science. Theories are fervently believed, but then discarded. This makes some wonder that if the certain truths of yesterday become the errors or even half-truths of today, the same might apply to the apparent successes of contemporary science. Could our present day 'knowledge' becomes tomorrow's 'falsehood'?

These are not trivial or frivolous questions. They live at the root of much scepticism about the claims of modern science, and have given rise to considerable research in the so-called sociology of science. That looks at the social influences on scientists, and considers how far their work is constrained by factors sometimes outside their knowledge and control. Science could be the mere product of place and time. 'Post-modernists' have repudiated the idea of a truth that exists across time. Truth becomes simply what people believe, and when people believe different things they have different truths. Different beliefs construct different realities. This relativism makes truth depend on who believes it, and when they do, so that there is our truth and their truth, and perhaps even my truth and your truth. This idea spells death to the notion of sound knowledge and the dispassionate exercise of human reason. It is a mortal threat to the conduct of science itself.

Many deny that there is any objective truth in areas such as morality and aesthetics. Yet once they start questioning the idea of truth in one area, it is easy to extend the same arguments to others. Science itself needs the idea of an objective truth as a goal, which is the same for everyone everywhere. It needs the idea of a reality that may not be fully understood, but is equally invariant. Any idea that science works, and that we do not have to think about the presuppositions of science, refuses to say what is meant by 'working' or what scientific 'success' is. We need assurance that, as humans, we can understand the world confronting us.

We have to face limitations on our knowledge, and the provisional nature of science. When we do, the idea that science can disprove the existence of God becomes problematic. Unless we define science as the source of all knowledge, we cannot say what ultimately can or cannot exist. People were once absolutely certain that an atom cannot be split. It once even seemed true by definition, and yet had to be repudiated. You can always stipulate anything by definition, saying, for example, that only matter exists. Materialists have often done just that, just as 'physicalists' and 'naturalists' in philosophy can make what is real depend on the edicts of physics, or perhaps a wider body of science. These are philosophical positions, not statements within science. They need philosophical justification, because they define reality in terms of the possibilities of human knowledge. Since it is true by definition that God transcends human knowledge, that would rule out God's existence. It rules out the possibility of even recognizing God's actions in our world, as the possibility of any divine origin is ignored. Such arbitrary decisions hardly constitute a rational approach, and ignore the necessity of giving science firm foundations, based on reason. Science does not deal with the whole of human experience, and cannot provide its own justification. Why should we trust it? When science is challenged, it has to look beyond its own resources for a defence. Narrowing the idea of evidence and reason to what happens within science makes it impossible to explain why we should practise science in the first place.

2

Are science and religion just different?

The autonomy of science?

Science tries to describe and explain physical events in the one world we all share. It follows that Christianity cannot, and should not, ignore it. We live in God's world, and that same world is the focus of scientific investigation. God is Creator. Science investigates His Creation. Science and religion, and Christianity in particular, must have much in common. Could they even support each other, or are they, as many are all too ready to point out, in conflict? Science should not rule out the relevance of any religion by definition, by making science the only source of knowledge. Even so, there would seem to be still plenty of ways in which science and religion could give rival accounts of the nature of the world, both of which cannot be right.

We must be wary of too readily accepting the long-established thesis of the intrinsic conflict between science and religion. It does not bear historical examination, in that, for instance, the founders of modern science in the seventeenth century were often motivated by a theistic understanding of the world. Scientists such as the great Isaac Newton, for example, rooted what they saw as 'natural philosophy' in a Book of Nature. They saw God as its Author, and the Book was considered to be as informative about God's world as that other Book, the Bible.[3] Newton declared that 'the most elegant system of the sun, planets and comets, would not have arisen without the design and dominion of an intelligent and powerful being'. Reference to God was as essential to his natural philosophy as the working of his mathematics. Many of the first participants of the Royal Society, the prestigious scientific institution in London founded in 1660, at the time of the restoration of the monarchy, were strongly motivated in their scientific research by belief in God. The slogan of a group of thinkers called the Cambridge Platonists, who influenced Newton, was 'Reason is the candle of the Lord'.[4] It was not regarded as a blinding searchlight, only a flickering and hesitant flame. Nevertheless, their trust in its illumination for the pursuit of human knowledge was grounded in religious faith.

As science has progressed, it has seen itself as increasingly autonomous and self-reliant. Scientific method has viewed appeals to supernatural intervention as at best irrelevant, and at worst to be condemned as superstitious. Either way, they got in the way of scientific progress. Human reason has often gloried in its own self-sufficiency, particularly during the eighteenth-century Enlightenment. In recent years, as we have seen in the case of postmodernism, the corrosive effects of relativism threaten the basis of science in such reason.

Some have taken scientific autonomy at face value, suggesting that science may be master in its own territory, but should not trespass on that of others. This attitude is expressed in popular language by the idea that faith is somehow completely different from matters of reason. It then becomes subjective, the mere property of individuals with no reference to the world. Scientific reason may still appear to tell the truth about the world while this mysterious characteristic called faith, that some appear to have and others do not, is said just to govern the attitudes of some individuals. Cynics even claim that faith is a distinctively religious state of mind that means believing something, *in spite of* the evidence. It goes with a refusal, it would be said, to acknowledge such evidence, and the existence of reasons that fail to support faith, or contradict it.

There are religious people who fit this description. There was the woman who refused to set foot in the Natural History Museum in London, on the grounds that seeing any pointers to evolution might shake her faith. Yet such an attitude cannot be sustained, once we recognize that faith is always faith in something that needs to be rationally specified, even if it has to go beyond our full understanding. Once we truly believe that this is God's world, its features must somehow reflect the will of that God. Religious faith may still produce its own problems. The venerable problems of evil and of suffering in the world spring to mind. A faith that exists in a vacuum, however, and is not founded on faith or trust in something or somebody is no faith at all. The minute we explain what we have faith in, or in whom we trust, we have to employ reason to describe it.

This can threaten those who ring-fence their faith against all conceivable challenges. Yet if nothing can count against what we believe, perhaps there is nothing that can count in its favour either. An empty faith that can never be challenged is also one that can never be supported. Faith that cannot be false cannot be true, because it does not seem to be about anything. Yet separating science and religion can still appear attractive, and not just to believers. Scientists may not want to get drawn into theological controversy, or may resent theological interference in science. It could just be that they feel it is discourteous to attack what some people hold dear. All in all, there are complex motivations at work. Some may think it just easier to say that science and religion deal with different categories of thought.

Do science and religion have different functions?

The idea that science and religion are just different has some truth on its side. Science does not deal with questions of meaning and purpose. It looks to how things happen, and is not interested in the ultimate question of why they do. The most basic question of all, namely why there is something rather than nothing, is outside the scope of science to answer. In the 1950s, a Christian physicist based in Oxford, Charles Coulson, followed current interpretations of subatomic phenomena and suggested that science and religion are complementary.[5] Just as one cannot simultaneously establish the position and momentum of an electron, he suggested that science and religion can examine the same reality from different perspectives, and come up with equally valid but different answers. Further back, in the 1920s, the philosopher

Alfred North Whitehead claimed that 'science is concerned with the general conditions which are observed to regulate physical phenomena, where religion is wholly wrapped up in the contemplation of moral and aesthetic values'. This suggests that religion has a significantly different function from the physical sciences, a view that has been echoed in modern science, for instance by the American biologist Stephen H. Gould.

Yet the distinction can come at a cost. We can quickly revert to an idea that science tells us how the world is, and religion deals with our personal reactions to and interpretation of it. Science is then about truth, and religion about stories or myths giving some guides for life. We are getting close to the slogan that says, 'If it isn't science, it's fiction'. Fiction can have its role in human life, and help us to understand human character. Choosing this as a model for the role of religion empties Christianity of the right to claim a truth about the world that is relevant for everyone.

In contemporary society, religion has often ceded the idea of truth to science. The more the functions of science and religion are distinguished, the more science becomes the custodian of truth. Religion is left with the role of telling stories that can inspire us but do not gain any grip on the real world. Religious belief is reduced to a determination to follow a certain, primarily ethical, way of life. Religious diversity in our world only helps this view, since it may seem that alternative ways of life are bolstered by entertaining different stories, whether about Moses, Christ, Muhammad, the Buddha or whoever. The function of religious doctrine is then merely to inspire commitments to various paths of action. We lose any idea that such commitment needs rational under-pinning by appeal to the nature of some objective reality.[6]

The idea that science is left as the custodian of truth will be challenged by relativists, linking truth to the beliefs of people. It is a paradox that the more religion is given a different function from science, the more science can gain prestige through the contrast, rather than itself being undermined. The constant danger is that we end by being unable to justify science or say why it is import-ant. The insulation of religion from science can be worked out at quite a high level philosophically. It is encouraged by the later work of Ludwig Wittgenstein, one of the most influential of all twentieth-century philosophers. He was much taken with the analogy between different uses of language and the different rules for different games. He talked of 'language-games'. His stress on the different uses of language leads to the view he held that meaning depends on context. It is what you do with language, rather than what it is apparently about, that matters. Some people could say that the function of sci-ence is to express facts, and the function of religion is to express values. This idea of alternative language-games, each with its own rules, can seem attractive. Science could not then judge religious claims any more than the rule of one game can be applied to another. If someone who is used to playing baseball has a go at cricket, it is no use hitting the ball and then hurling the bat down and running to the fielder in the covers, as if he was at first base. Similarly, picking up the ball in soccer and running with it constitutes, as it once historically did, the forma-tion of a different game with different rules.

Does this analogy cast light on the nature of scientific and religious claims? Is looking for scientific evidence for religious truth, or seeking purpose in scientific causation, a confusion of logical categories? The rules of one could be said to have been misapplied to the other. There is enough truth in this view to make some embrace it. Traditional scientific method – developing theories through observation and experiment – is clearly not appropriate for faith. Further, science demands provisional acceptance of theories, with a recognition that they may very well be later shown to be wrong or incomplete. Perhaps scientific detachment is different from the deep commitment demonstrated by many religious believers. That, though, can be stressed too much. Scientists can become very committed to the truth of their theories, and may resist giving them up even in the face of apparently contrary evidence. Perseverance with a theory may bring greater insight even if it has eventually to be modified. Their stubbornness may bring results, and giving up a theory could leave them without any guide to future research. Similarly, a Christian believer totally committed to the truth of Christianity and living accordingly may realize that while there may be apparent reasons not to believe, it is more sensible to strive to understand more about their faith.

Fencing off science from Christian belief may make Christians feel safe. Yet if both are really concerned with what is true, the beliefs of each may be relevant to the other. As long as the two are encouraged to exist in parallel with each other, but never meeting, the issue of truth is not confronted. If both are in some sense true, how do they relate to each other? If neither are true, science itself becomes fatally damaged. If only science is said to be about truth and religion is about something else the pre-eminence of science and the irrelevance of religion may have been achieved by empty definition.

It is likely that this world is imbued with meaning and purpose, if it is God's Creation. Some things may have an intrinsic value, and some actions may be intrinsically evil. Claims to such truth have as much universal import as any scientific discovery. For instance, humans are typically said by various charters of human rights, such as the United Nations Universal Declaration of Human Rights, to have an inherent dignity. It may be difficult to justify this assertion without claiming that this dignity has been conferred by God. In any case, wherever the universality of natural human rights is proclaimed, we are talking about an objective truth that is no less true for being beyond the scope of empirical science.

The role of reason

Science depends for its success on the exercise of human reason. Scientists may sometimes claim to explain this by talking of a causal account of reason, involving neural pathways in the brain or suchlike. We are, it may be said, just elaborate computers, programmed to operate in particular ways. This is a popular comparison, which follows a long tradition of comparing the human mind to whatever is the latest product of human technology. The model was once a clockwork mechanism, which when wound up was bound to go on in a certain way. That was a popular theme in the seventeenth and eighteenth centuries.

Nowadays we recognize that the physical world is much more complicated and unpredictable than that. Different models are brought into play. Yet even computers have to be programmed by somebody. However complex they become, and however much their operation seems to outstrip the capabilities of the human mind, their purposes, and the rules by which they operate, have to be set for them by humans. The results they produce have to be interpreted. They are not replacements for the human mind, but extensions of it.

There is a basic difference between being able to reason, and hence recognize truth, and simply being caused to operate in ways that may or may not accidentally lead to our attaining truth. Without an ability to stand back and assess evidence, and consider whether scientific or other beliefs are justified, we are just haphazardly conditioned to come to believe things. It becomes a matter of luck if we are right, and we will never be in a position to know. Some make an appeal to evolution to show how we have evolved to accept certain useful beliefs as true, and other more dangerous ones as false. If we do not fear lions, we are liable to be eaten by them. If we do not see holes, we are liable to fall into them. Humans have obviously evolved to attempt to avoid such dangers naturally. Yet even if elements of our common human nature can be explained through this evolutionary heritage, explaining everything in that manner will still be self-defeating.

The theory of evolution is a theory within science. It may have considerable empirical support, and Christians should not fear it. If they truly believe that all is in God's hands as the ultimate Creator of everything, they need not have preconceived ideas about how the world must have developed, or evolved. Yet scientists, too, have to use their rational abilities to assess evolutionary theory and its scope. The claims of the theory presuppose a human ability to use reason to recognize what is true. If humans have just evolved to believe in the theory of evolution, there could be no reason to trust it. We may accidentally have hit on the truth or we may not. We would not be in any position to assess our position rationally. If the theory were true, according to its own lights it would just be its usefulness in helping us to survive and reproduce that makes us believe it.

The very persuasiveness of modern science depends on a view of human reason that has to go beyond science itself. Religion itself should not ignore science, if we realize that this is God's world. Science, though, cannot exist in its own bubble, but needs presuppositions that have to be grounded elsewhere. The most central of these is a trust in human reason that is not conditioned by circumstance, physiology or whatever. Giving science its own sphere of influence and restricting its ability to criticize religion, morality or other realms of human activity, may seem to set everyone free. In fact, it leaves science itself ungrounded. While science may not then criticize non-scientific positions, it is cast adrift, unable to appeal to any rational principles or objective truth, that are external to its own practices. Its inability to criticize Christianity is mirrored by its own inability to justify itself.

There may be significant topics where the possibility of conflict cannot be ruled out. Arguments rage in sensitive areas concerning various origins. Is the Big Bang at the origin of the universe relevant to the idea of Creation? Is there a fundamental distinction between life and physical entities, and would it matter if there were not? Are humans radically different from other animals, including the higher apes? Is human consciousness special, or is it really no different from what happens in a computer? The role of God in the world, and the place in it of humans and their characteristics, are issues that are thrown into relief by the onward march of science. Pretending that they can by definition have no impact on Christian faith is a refusal to use our reason to face up to the reality of the world in which we are placed. Yet we must not saw off the branch we are sitting on. We cannot explain away human rationality without undermining the possibility of science as a reliable path to truth. The idea that 'reason is the candle of the Lord' is a powerful stimulus for respecting and trusting in science.

3

Could science support Christianity?

The 'anthropic principle'

If science and Christian faith both attempt to deal with the same world, it is wrong to insulate them from each other. Could they therefore not conflict, but actually on occasion support one another? It is fanciful to suppose that science can prove the truth of any religious faith any more than it can disprove it. This is not just because its methodology and purposes are significantly different. Science is not in the business of proof, in the sense that mathematics or geometry is. It puts forward theories that have to be held tentatively until all the facts are in, and for humans, that may be never, in this life. We cannot attain omniscience. Even a fundamental scientific theory has to be held as a matter of faith, however strongly held. Contrary evidence may always be forthcoming, as Karl Popper pointed out when he showed the impossibility of proving that all swans are white. There may always be a black swan about to be discovered.

Even if science is not in the business of logical proof, it can provide pointers to truth. A Christian would believe that God's world is shot through with His purposes. God's transcendence means that we may not wholly grasp His ways, but as we investigate the physical world, it would be strange if we did not see reflections of His will. The discipline of natural theology, looking from the world towards God, bears witness to this. It has had a strong influence through the centuries on English theology. The beauty of the world, and its apparent intricate design, has led many thinkers to see the world as God's Creation. Even Charles Darwin, who ended up as an agnostic, was motivated to produce his theory of evolution by the theological argument for the existence of God from the apparent design observed in the biological world.

In more recent years, some biologists have used the theory of evolution to explain natural development and change without God. That has not destroyed the argument about design, but displaced it to a higher level. This was dramatized in the middle 1970s by the appeal in physics to the so-called 'anthropic principle'. John Wheeler was a Princeton physicist who had been a pupil of Einstein, and was the originator of the phrase 'black hole' in cosmology. He posed the question why the universe is so large, and claimed that it was 'because we are here'.[7] He was not making a religious statement about God's design, but was pointing out that the nature of the universe is such that carbon-based life, such as that of humans, could not be produced quickly. The size of the universe is linked to its time in existence. Carbon is produced by the death of stars, and would not exist in a young universe. This is one of many features of our universe that give rise to wonder. The cosmos must not expand too fast, or too slowly, and must have the right mix of forces for stars to burn for billions of years but then die out with a bang. We are told that 'they are both the producer and distributor of elements'.[8] The existence of stars that are stable, but not perfectly so, appears to be one of many 'fine-tuned' properties of the universe.

The nearer we get to the absolute beginning of the universe, the more instances we find of such fine-tuning among the initial conditions that made the development of the universe possible. It has to have a life-supporting number of dimensions, and display a regularity and stability in its processes that make life possible. One estimate is that there are 30 constants in basic physics and modern cosmology that must be fine-tuned for the emergence of life. Without life there would be no observers and no physics. The anthropic principle holds that any scientific account of the conditions necessary for the existence of the universe has to allow for the existence of observers at some stage. Otherwise our own physics does not allow for our own existence.

This can be made into a trivial truth. We would not exist in a different kind of universe. Perhaps it is not surprising that we exist in the one we do. Yet taking this for granted, and feeling that it needs no explanation, is hardly a scientific attitude. It should be surprising that of all the possible initial conditions at the beginning of the developing universe, everything was so evenly balanced as to make our life possible. To take one example, the initial density of the universe was on a knife-edge between tremendous expansion or catastrophic collapse for a nanosecond after the Big Bang. The density was unimaginably high (around 10 to the power of 24 kilograms per cubic metre).[9] If it were only a single kilogram per cubic metre higher, the universe would already have collapsed. This example can be multiplied many times. A general moral is that the characteristics of our universe, including our own existence, are tied up with enormously precise initial conditions. Our existence on an apparently insignificant planet is bound up with the basic constitution of the universe.

The 'God of the gaps'

Some see these scientific accounts as pointing to a divine purpose. Yet it is no part of modern science to wonder why things happen. To many scientists, attributing divine agency to events seems to be just giving up on science. It seems as facile as our trying to explain something by saying 'the fairies did it', and be absolved from looking for any further explanation. That stops scientific progress. The history of science demonstrates how a readiness to look at natural events in their own terms, rather than attributing external personal agency, has reaped results. Thunder and lightning are given natural physical explanations rather than relying on an appeal to Zeus, as the ancient Greeks did. We do not need to explain the behaviour of the sea by appeal to the Greek god Poseidon, or in Roman times Neptune. The first Greek thinkers to look at the physical world in its own terms were able to avoid talk of the gods in this manner, and instead claimed that everything could be explained in terms of natural elements such as earth, air, fire or water or some combination of these. The elements could often appear to be agents of change in themselves. Water could be seen as a liquid, solid when frozen, or vapour when boiling. Ancient thinkers went on to see basic matter in more sophisticated terms. They talked of atoms, which by definition could not be divided further but combined in different ways to form different kinds of objects. Thus a basic materialism explained the nature of things. Only over the last century has the nature of matter been seen as even more mysterious, composed of subatomic particles, some of which are virtually undetectable even with modern instruments. Matter has been dissolved into a more intangible combination of forces, and fields. It has become much more difficult to define what a materialist really believes in.

Some allege that this historical story of the advance of science means that God has no role in our understanding of the world. It is certainly fruitful to investigate the physical world in physical terms. There is, though, a short step from the scientific focus of scientific method on the natural world to a denial of the value of any explanation from outside science. 'Methodological naturalism' can change from being a view about the scope of scientific method to an avowedly metaphysical denial of any 'supernatural' explanation. We have quickly gone from human knowledge, through the application of science now or in the future, to the nature of reality itself. That is a major change of subject.

We must beware, too, of allowing the idea of God as Creator to trade on present gaps in our knowledge. Such gaps may always be filled, as they have been in the past. Yet we should not assume too easily that all such gaps will inevitably be filled. That is a philosophical position, with much in common with traditional materialism. Just as one should not be too ready to rush in with an appeal to divine intervention every time something seems impossible to explain, it goes far beyond the scope of science into the realms of philosophy to say that there can be no such thing as God's action in the world. Even so, an appeal to the existence of God through gaps in our knowledge is strangely inadequate. The Oxford physicist Charles Coulson said in the 1950s:[10] 'Either God is in the whole of nature, with no gaps, or He is not there at all.' A Christian believer has to accept that the whole world has its origins in God, and that all of it is sustained by Him. It must be under God's control, and somehow reflect His existence. He does not just tweak little bits here and there.

Some scientists attempt to block any theistic explanation for cosmic coincidences by trying to find an explanation within the bounds of science. They see that the exceptionally narrow range of initial conditions at the start of our universe, which allowed rational beings to develop, is extraordinary. One possibility would be metaphorically to shrug one's shoulders and say that as we could not exist in another kind of universe, it is just a brute fact that we are here. That stops all explanation. One genuine attempt at explanation is to say, on the basis of mathematics, that all physical possibilities have to exist. We then live in one of an infinite number of universes, each with different initial conditions and different physical laws. This, though, is not much better than just saying that that is how it is. The fact that we exist shows it must be possible, and that is all we can know.

This idea of a multi-verse is much talked about, but if other universes are by definition beyond our reach, and of unimaginable physical constitution, we seem to be postulating entities that transcend our knowledge every bit as much as God. The very idea of their physical nature is so distant from our idea of physics that it is difficult to see what we even mean by using the word 'physical' in such a context. If God can and does reveal Himself in the workings of this world, inaccessible universes are far more remote. There may or may not be such universes, but their possible existence is as much a subject of reasoned speculation beyond the reach of empirical science as any talk of a Mind underlying everything.

Is religion 'natural'?

The anthropic principle appears to point to a direction in physical reality from the moment of what many would see as Creation. Arguments about this have to go beyond science itself. It is an intriguing fact that contemporary research in the new discipline of the cognitive science of religion has pointed to how religious impulses seem to be deeply rooted in human nature.[11] In particular, it underlines how humans naturally look for purpose in the physical world. This may be conducive to evolutionary advantage. We can hear a noise in the forest and assume it is caused by an agent, perhaps an animal stalking us. Research suggests that if we cannot observe the agent, humans are remarkably ready to assume an explanation through immaterial agency by spirits, gods or whatever. The urge to find why things happen also seems deeply rooted, and it is much easier to assume that things happen for a purpose. When dreadful tragedies occur in life, we still seem naturally driven to ask 'why'.

Small children find it easier to give explanations in terms of purpose than with a more sophisticated scientific explanation. When asked why rocks may be pointed, they are far more likely to say something like 'so that birds cannot sit on them' than refer to a process like erosion. Even adults can find arguments from design much easier to grasp than more complicated accounts of evolution. Scientific reasoning is a difficult intellectual achievement, which when done properly requires years of training. In that, it is not unlike theology, itself an intellectual discipline that can be very complex. Neither are on a par with straightforward religious faith, such as that of a child.

Experiments with children even show that, as their minds develop, they find it easy to think in terms of God. They can understand by the age of four that their mother cannot know everything. At the age of three, if they hide something, such as an apple under a cup, they may easily assume that their mother knows its new place, even though she did not see it moved. A year later, they know that their mother's perspective is different from their own, and that she does not know everything. She may not even know what they do. They develop what psychologists call a 'theory of mind'. Yet when asked if God knows where the apple is, children find it easy to go on assuming that 'God knows everything', or because 'God is God' (both quotes from four-year-olds). Some may retort that this merely reflects how the children have been brought up, but that is not the point. The moral is how easy it is for a child to go on thinking about God's full knowledge even as they come to understand human limitations. The idea of someone who knows everything is not strange to them. It is natural for them to think in that way.

There are many other examples of how the human mind seems naturally inclined to religious understanding, and finds it easy to latch on to religious beliefs. Ideas of mind apart from body, and of the person continuing after death, are deeply rooted in human nature. The cognitive science of religion draws on child psychology and anthropology to show the universality of religious impulses. It can link up with evolutionary biology to show how these traits could have become established in human nature. However religious impulses become entrenched, they are there, as a force to be reckoned with. Religion is not a private optional extra for some odd humans, but must be recognized as a universal characteristic to be reckoned with in public life. Its roots lie deep in what it is to be human. Even when regimes try to expunge it, as happened in Communist Eastern Europe, it will eventually re-emerge.

The universality of religion may be demonstrated, but human nature does not decide the kind of religion practised. We may search for divinity, but this takes different forms. We are ready to think of gods, perhaps even one God, but know little of His nature. That should not surprise Christians, since the whole point of the Christian gospel is that God has revealed His nature to us in human terms that we can understand. Christianity has never believed that pure reason is sufficient for faith, although it can underpin it. The light of reason may be God-given, but we also need more specific revelation to guide us. The cognitive science of religion shows that there is a 'God-shaped hole' in our understanding, even if we need more specific divine revelation. God may sometimes seem hidden from us, but our nature gives us a bias to some form of religious faith.

Why, then, does everyone not have a religious belief? Atheists may well accept that there is a biologically based urge to believe, but still maintain that it is an infantile outlook we have to grow out of. As we use our reason, they would claim, we can see its inadequacy. Nothing can be deduced about the truth of any religion from our propensity to think in religious terms. Some scientists will go further, and explain away all religious belief on the grounds that it has just accidentally developed through evolution. Such belief could be advantageous through evolution but, it may be suggested, be a by-product of other advantageous human traits. Some see explaining away all religious faith like this as the ultimate victory of science over religion. Yet it is just as easy to view our tendencies to see things in religious terms as God-given. As humans, we have to use reason, and we can make a cumulative case for the rationality of the Christian faith. The cognitive science of religion shows that the roots of religious belief are too deep in our common human nature to be discarded simply by some definition that says they produce unscientific beliefs. The very reason that lies at the root of all science, and even produces the discipline of the cognitive science of religion, has to be brought into play. That reason cannot itself be explained away without disastrous consequences for science itself.

4

Does science need Christianity?

God's world

Science and religion give accounts of the same world, even if they often answer different questions. What modern science says is important for anyone who believes that this is God's world, but it has sometimes been too ready to bask in its own success. Its achievements are literally tangible, in that we can now manipulate much of physical reality around us and, within limits, predict its behaviour. 'Science works', and produces agreed results in a way that theology, and indeed philosophy, do not seem to.

What presuppositions does science bring to its task? Why should it be confident of its success? Perhaps, in our small part of the universe, we live in a pool of order within a vast ocean of disorder. How can we be so confident of using the known to predict what is presently unknown, going from here to there, or now to then? Why should science generalize from what it can observe to what it cannot? This is the issue of the universality of science, in that physical laws are regarded as constant and universal. Yet there is a problem of how we can be sure that our familiar physical laws can still apply to inaccessible events at the far limits of an expanding universe. The problem is magnified if we talk of alternative universes.

This universal reach of science is an integral part of its assumed success. Yet the eighteenth-century philosopher David Hume was reluctant to base reasoning on anything but present experience. He could not be sure that the future would be like the past, or even that the sun will rise tomorrow as it always has. Hume's solution was that we simply expect the future to be the same, but that is a psychological explanation, for which he could give no rational grounding. Any philosophy based on human experience will come up against the same difficulty, and conclude that science is based on hope not reason. We predict what experiences we may expect to have, without any rational grounding for the prediction. Hume's predicament, like that of many following him in the modern era, was a result of his unwillingness to invoke God as a grounding for anything. Yet the notion of God as the source of human reason had given seventeenth-century science the confidence to build up its knowledge of the world. Science was able to discover natural regularities, it was thought, because it recognized laws ordained by the ultimate lawgiver, God. It could give insights not just into how the world happens to function here and now, but into how God's world functions everywhere at all times.

The idea of law may suggest rules that can never be broken. Yet science need only assume that physical processes are normally regular, orderly and stable. Modern physics shows that statistical regularities can be produced by unpredictable and even random behaviour at the level of subatomic particles. It is also a matter of everyday experience that human beings possess a freedom to behave in ways that may not be completely determined or predictable. Modern science transcends the mechanistic world, as envisaged by Isaac Newton. Its recognition of deep regularities in nature does not entail thinking that everything is governed by iron-clad necessity. As we have seen, even the process of scientific investigation requires a freedom that can enable scientists to rise above their own circumstances. Freedom and reason go together.

Christian doctrines about human nature and free will underpin the very possibility of doing science. Our freedom and rationality are gifts of God. Otherwise, making scientific investigations part of a remorseless series of cause and effect undermines the whole idea of scientific explanation. Any explanation must itself be scientifically explained. That produces an explanation that cannot be taken at face value, but demands further causal explanation, and so on for ever in an infinite regress. There is no escape from trusting our ability to reason and grasp truth in the first place. Unless our rationality can rise above the constraints of time and place, the ability of human beings to do science at all is put into question.

Another conclusion that arises from the Christian understanding of God's role is that the world does not have to be as it is. It is, in philosophical jargon, 'contingent' – not necessary. God, as Creator, did not have to create it as it is. There are other possible worlds. As the multi-verse idea bears witness, some physicists believe that such worlds exist. However that may be, modern science arose from the realization that armchair science was not an option. Ancient philosophers such as Aristotle were prone to think about what has to be the case, even when recognizing the importance of observation. They worked from first principles. The world had to be eternal, and there could be no other worlds. The heavenly bodies moved in circles, because circles embody perfection. Modern science, however, emphasized the role of observation and experiment in seeing what properties happen to be the case, not what should be. A rational God would produce a certain coherence, stability and regularity in natural events, but God's own freedom is restricted if the nature of the world is necessary, so that the physical world has to be as it is. The whole edifice of modern science demonstrates that we cannot work out what kind of world we actually inhabit without looking at it. Physicists, who rely on mathematics to build assumptions about a multiplicity of possible worlds, merely show how mathematics alone is insufficient. We have to find out what actually happens.

God and reason

Science has to make assumptions about the nature of the world that presuppose the efficacy of experimental method. Its purpose is to find out how the world happens to be, not how it must be. The world is broadly predictable, but nothing happens of necessity. The Christian idea of a God who has freely chosen to create this kind of world, but does so in a rational way, gives warrant for these views. Our world is the result of the will of a Creator who is the source of the very rationality that scientists rely on. We do not have to be surprised when, at the microscopic level described in quantum mechanics, we find that the world is not as predictable or blindly mechanistic as was once argued for. Yet we can assume that science can discover a level of order and regularity open to the discovery of science because everything is the product of the rational Mind underlying everything. Our own freedom, according to Christian doctrine, reflects the freedom exhibited in the mind of God. We are made in His image. Albert Einstein, the most famous scientist of the twentieth century, maintained that 'the eternally incomprehensible thing about the world is its comprehensibility'. Science dare not take this for granted, but a Christian does not have to accept Einstein's judgement that the issue is eternally incomprehensible. Its very intelligibility is linked to the deliberate Creation by God who had his own purposes for humans.

Mathematics is an illustration of how the workings of the human mind can in a mysterious manner unlock the secrets of the physical universe. At first sight, mathematics might seem no more than an elaborate system of symbols, with inbuilt rules. It might even appear like an elaborate game, such as chess, but on a larger scale. Perhaps the human mind relishes constructing elaborate intellectual structures for their own sake. Yet mathematics latches on to the workings of the physical world in a remarkable way. The advent of ever more elaborate computers, as adjuncts to the human mind, enables us to expand our reach further. Why should mathematics be not only internally consistent but reflect an order in the world, so that it can somehow describe the way the physical world works? This is another illustration of how human reason can understand a physical reality that has its own rational structure. Yet we should never take for granted our human ability to understand the intricate workings of vast regions of the universe.

When St John, in the first verse of his Gospel, talks of a 'logos', saying that 'in the beginning was the logos', he meant far more than 'word', as translations usually have it. The Greek word *logos* is the root of our word 'logic', and expresses a concept resonating through ancient Greek philosophy, up to New Testament times. The earliest philosophers, even before the time of Socrates, saw the 'logos' as a rational principle underlying everything. It could hold in balance opposites such as hot and cold, or wet and dry. The meaning expanded so that Plato was able to assume that 'logos' meant not just a principle within the physical world but our ability to explain the basis of our knowledge. It came to cover both the reason inherent within the world and the human reason that understood it. St John linked the term with the idea of God, saying that 'the logos was with God and the logos was God'. These familiar words, linked to the Christmas story, are of tremendous significance. The very reason that makes the practice of science possible is linked to the inherent rationality of the Creator through whom all things were made, and also with the revelation of God in Jesus.

Many would vehemently want to defend the autonomy of the scientific enterprise, and its independence from any theology. Some might admit that seventeenth-century science was influenced by Christian understandings but would argue that the historical origins of science are irrelevant to its contemporary justification. Even so, once we discard theology, we still have to explain the order that according to the presuppositions of science prevails throughout the physical universe. The mantra 'science works' is a poor defence against those who attack its right to claim any truth.

Science gives us the power to destroy our world, and we cannot shirk the question as to why we should participate in its practice, or put any trust in it. There is the pervading moral question about how we should use the knowledge we gain. Science cannot answer any of these challenges on its own. We must stand outside science to defend it rationally, and decide how it should be used. Once we repudiate the belief in God that helped found modern science, we can leave science floundering. Some may even feel free to ignore its findings, blaming it for many of the ills of the present world. That denigration of scientific knowledge takes us rapidly towards nihilism, according to which nothing matters, because nothing is true.

Science can convey the wonder that comes in the investigation of the intricate beauty of the workings of the physical world. That can be reflected in the elegance of a mathematical formula that helps us grasp the rational comprehensibility of the universe. This points to a truth that lies beyond human beings and has its source in God. The understanding that this is God's world can motivate scientists through the realization that there is a truth to be discovered. They may even realize that in a humble way they are thinking God's thoughts after Him. That is the reverse of the idea that religion conflicts with science. It underpins it, and can motivate scientists in their research. Christians are assured that because we are made in God's image we can in part grasp the nature of God's world.

Linking science to wider Christian beliefs means that we are freed from the artificial distinction between scientific facts and subjective values. What happens in the world, and what ought to happen for its inhabitants to flourish, are linked. The investigation of causal events within the physical world must not be separated from the question of an ultimate divine purpose for it. Both are in the widest sense 'facts'. The inherent dignity of human beings should be considered as much a matter of truth as any claims made by a physical theory.

Science plays a crucial role in modern human life, but needs direction. Deciding what scientific research is important, and worth pursuing, involves judgements that have to be guided by principles that come from beyond science. A 'neutral' science, pursued in a vacuum and freed of all so-called 'values', is dangerous. It lacks direction, but is also ultimately pointless. The idea of an objective truth that gives science its purpose has to come from beyond science. Science loses its bearings when detached from other forms of rational understanding, including religious belief. Scientific understanding is blind if it relies only on its own resources. So, far from undermining religious faith, it needs some of the insights that such faith can provide.

Notes

1 See Roger Trigg, *Beyond Matter: Why Science Needs Metaphysics*, West Conshohocken, PA: Templeton Press, 2015, pp. 6ff.

2 Thomas S. Kuhn, *The Structure of Scientific Revolutions*, Chicago, IL: Chicago University Press, 1962, Chapter X, pp. 110ff.

3 See John Hedley Brooke, *Science and Religion: Some Historical Perspectives*, Cambridge: Cambridge University Press, 1991, 2014.

4 See C. Taliaferro and A. J. Teply, *Cambridge Platonist Spirituality*, Mahwah, NJ: Paulist Press, 2004.

5 C. A. Coulson, *Science and Christian Belief*, Oxford: Oxford University Press, 1955, pp. 67ff.

6 See Roger Trigg, *Reason and Commitment*, Cambridge: Cambridge University Press, 1973.

7 J. A. Wheeler, 'Genesis and Observership', in R. E. Butts and J. Hintikka (eds), *Foundational Problems in the Special Sciences*, Dordrecht: Reidel, 1977, p. 18.

8 Geraint F. Lewis and Luke A. Barnes, *A Fortunate Universe: Life in a Finely Tuned Cosmos*, Cambridge: Cambridge University Press, 2016, p. 112.

9 Lewis and Barnes, *Fortunate Universe*, p. 167.

10 Coulson, *Science and Christian Belief*, p. 22.

11 See Roger Trigg and Justin L. Barrett (eds), *The Roots of Religion: Explaining the Cognitive Science of Religion*, Farnham: Ashgate, 2014.

Further reading

Barrett, Justin L., *Born Believers: The Science of Children's Religious Belief*. New York: Free Press, 2012.

Brooke, John Hedley, *Science and Religion: Some Historical Perspectives*. Cambridge: Cambridge University Press, 1991, 2014.

Holder, Rodney, *Big Bang, Big God: A Universe Designed for Life?* Oxford: Lion Hudson, 2013.

Trigg, Roger, *Religion in Public Life*. Oxford: Oxford University Press, 2007.

Trigg, Roger, *Equality, Freedom and Religion*. Oxford: Oxford University Press, 2012.

Trigg, Roger, *Religious Diversity*. Cambridge: Cambridge University Press, 2014.

Trigg, Roger, *Beyond Matter: Why Science Needs Metaphysics*. West Conshohocken, PA: Templeton Press, 2015.